Amazing Animals

Written by Betsy Franco
Illustrated by Jesse Reisch

Children's Press®
A Division of Scholastic Inc.
New York • Toronto • London • Auckland • Sydney
Mexico City • New Delhi • Hong Kong
Danbury, Connecticut

For Tom
—B.F.

To all sentient beings
—J.R.

Reading Consultants

Linda Cornwell
Literacy Specialist

Katharine A. Kane
Education Consultant
(Retired, San Diego County Office of Education
and San Diego State University)

Jan Jenner, Ph.D.
Science Consultant

Library of Congress Cataloging-in-Publication Data
Franco, Betsy.
Amazing animals / written by Betsy Franco ; illustrated by Jesse Reisch.
p. cm. — (Rookie reader)
Summary: Briefly notes amazing animal actions such as a walrus feeling with its whiskers and a fly tasting with its feet.
ISBN 0-516-22263-5 (lib. bdg.) 0-516-27385-X (pbk.)
[1. Animals—Miscellanea—Juvenile literature. [1. Animals—Miscellanea.] I. Reisch, Jesse, ill. II. Title. III. Series.
QL49.F825 2002
590—dc21 2001047202

Printed in the United States of America.
1 2 3 4 5 6 7 8 9 10 R 11 10 09 08 07 06 05 04 03 02

A frog catches insects
with its tongue.

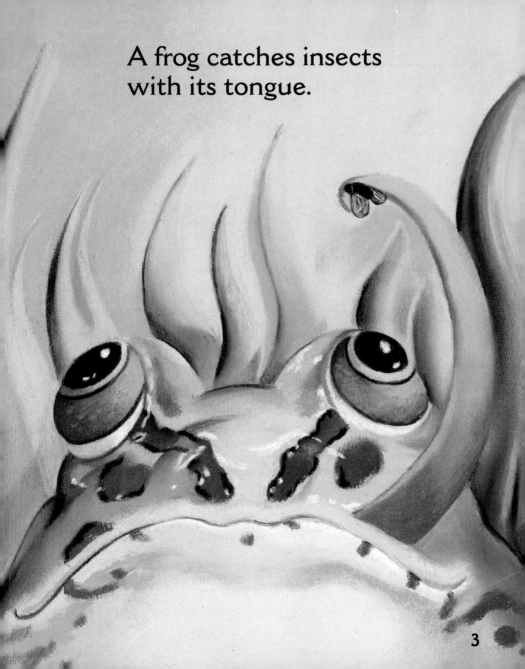

3

Its quick tongue is very sticky!

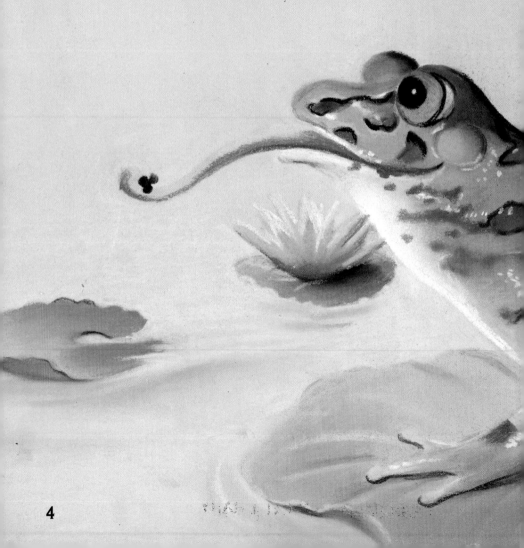

5

A fly tastes with its feet.

It tastes a treat
with the hairs on its feet.

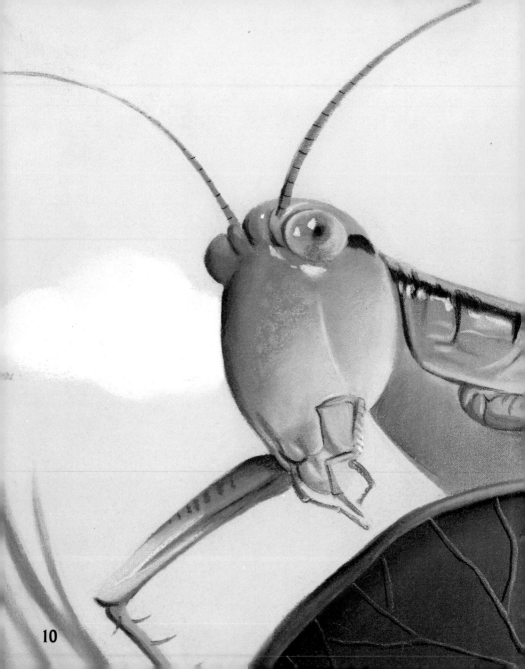
10

It rubs its leg on its wing
to make a special sound.

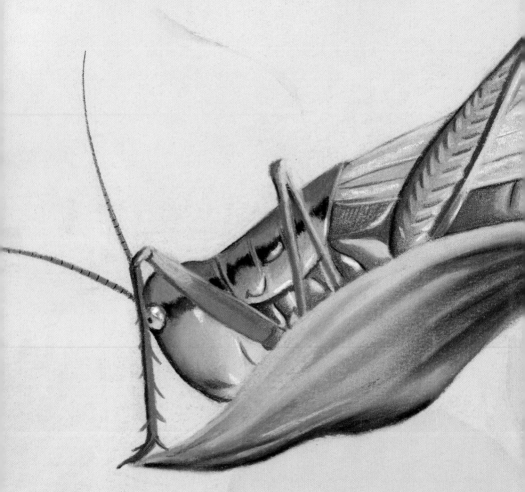

13

A walrus feels with its whiskers.

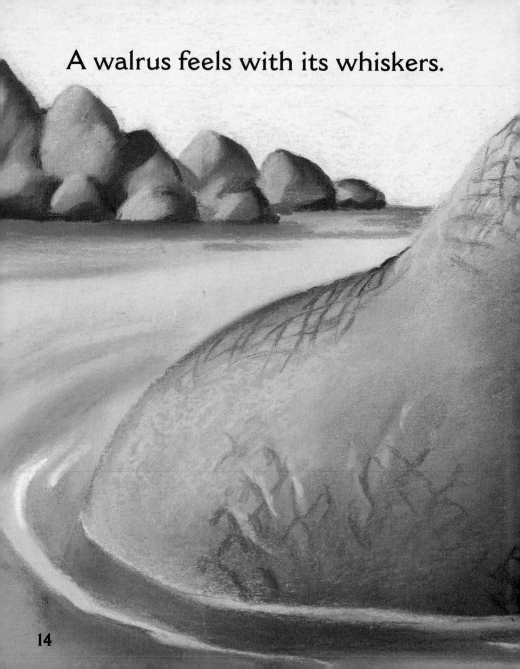

It knows when it finds
a rock or a meal!

17

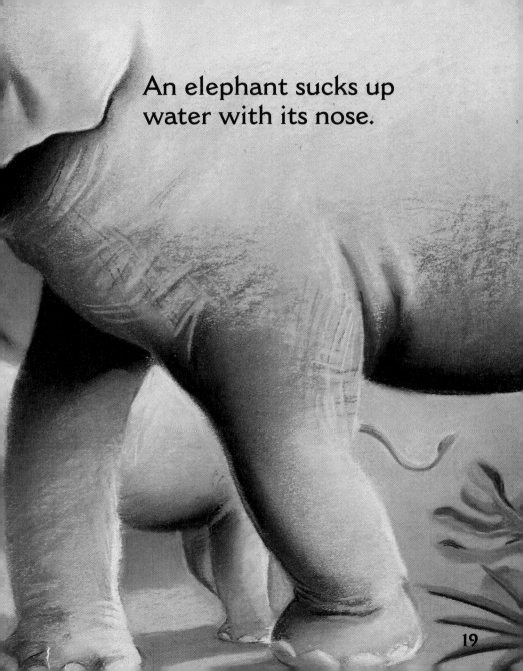

An elephant sucks up
water with its nose.

A grasshopper makes music
by rubbing its leg
up and down.

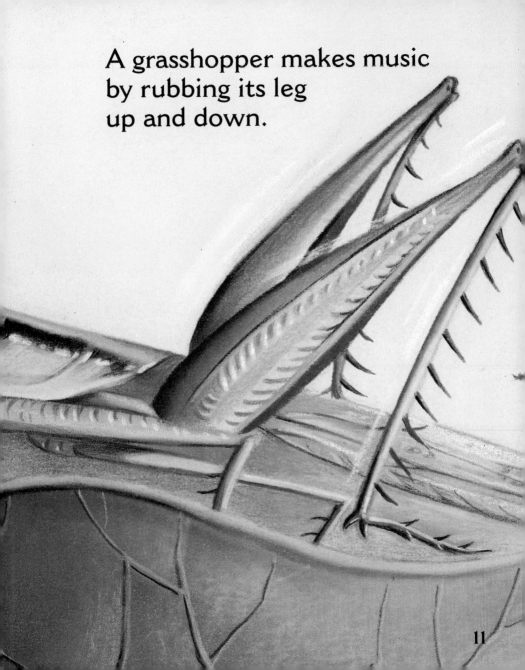

20

It squirts water into
its mouth like a hose.

An ant smells with its feelers.

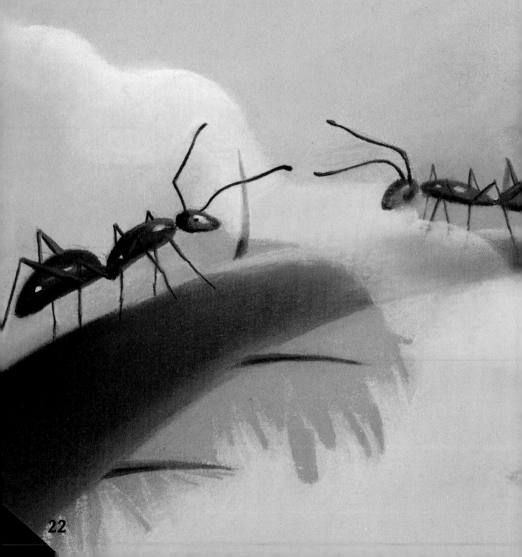

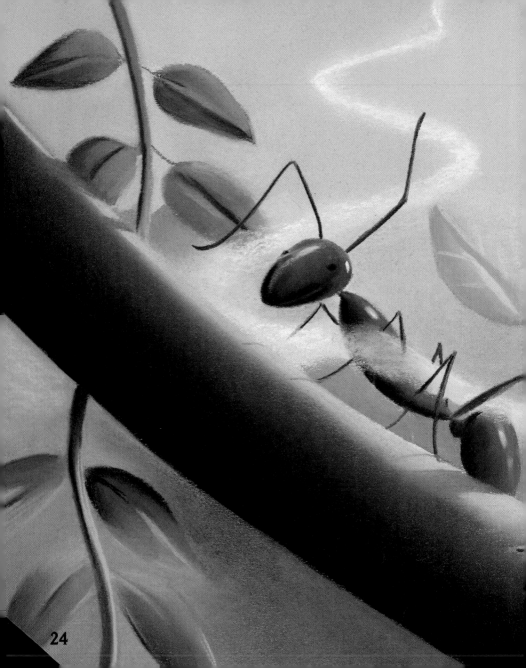

Its feelers up there
help it smell in the air.

A bee tells stories by dancing.

27

Its dance tells how far
the best flowers are.

Now you can see
how amazing animals can be!

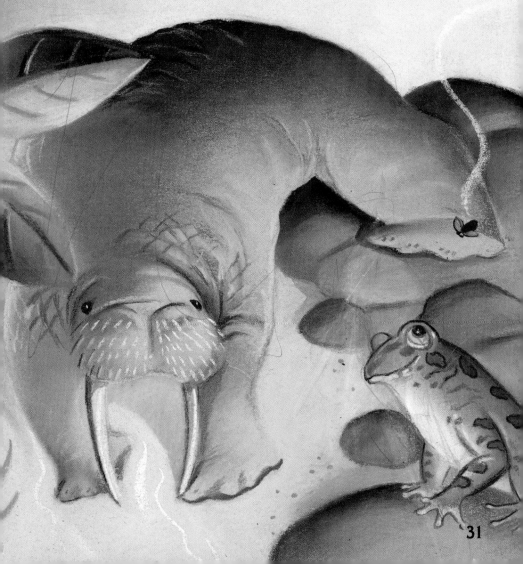

Word List (78 words)

a	down	insects	or	the
air	elephant	into	quick	there
amazing	far	is	rock	to
an	feelers	it	rubbing	tongue
and	feels	its	rubs	treat
animals	feet	knows	see	up
ant	finds	leg	smell	very
are	flowers	like	smells	walrus
be	fly	make	sound	water
bee	frog	makes	special	when
best	grasshopper	meal	squirts	whiskers
by	hairs	mouth	sticky	wing
can	help	music	stories	with
catches	hose	nose	sucks	you
dance	how	now	tastes	
dancing	in	on	tells	

About the Author

Betsy Franco lives in Palo Alto, California, where she has written more than forty books for children—picture books, poetry, and non-fiction. Betsy is the only female in her family, which includes her husband Douglas, her three sons James, Thomas, and David, and Lincoln the cat. She starts writing in the wee hours of the morning when everyone but Lincoln is asleep.

About the Illustrator

Jesse Reisch grew up in the Midwest, but wanted to live on more exotic shores. At an early age, it was clear to everyone that she loved art, but it would not be until she traveled the world and then moved to the San Francisco Bay area that she truly became an artist. She illustrates children's books and many other kinds of publications.